STEM

Building Tiny Houses

Compose and Decompose Shapes

Georgia Beth

Consultant

Lorrie McConnell, M.A.
Professional Development Specialist TK–12
Moreno Valley USD, CA

Publishing Credits

Rachelle Cracchiolo, M.S.Ed., *Publisher*
Conni Medina, M.A.Ed., *Managing Editor*
Dona Herweck Rice, *Series Developer*
Emily R. Smith, M.A.Ed., *Series Developer*
Diana Kenney, M.A.Ed., NBCT, *Content Director*
June Kikuchi, *Content Director*
Stacy Monsman, M.A., *Editor*
Michelle Jovin, M.A., *Assistant Editor*
Fabiola Sepulveda, *Graphic Designer*

Image Credits: front cover, p.1 Nadine Mitchell/Alamy; back cover Paul Moseley/MCT/Newscom; p.5 ZCHE/New Frontier Tiny Homes (Supplied by WENN)/Newscom; p.7 Tiny House Expedition/Rex Shutterstock; p.8 Paul Moseley/Star-Telegram via AP; p.14 Kenneth K. Lam/MCT/Newscom; p.16 ZCHE/New Frontier Tiny Homes/Supplied by WENN/Newscom; p.17 Benjamin Benschneider/MCT/Newscom; pp.18–19 Nikola Nastasic; pp.20, 21 ZCHD/Supplied by WENN/Newscom; pp.24–25 Photo by James Alfred Photography, courtesy of Mint Tiny House Company; p.27 Paul Zinken/picture-alliance/dpa/AP Images; p.29 Kuimet/Newscom; all other images iStock and/or Shutterstock.

Library of Congress Cataloging-in-Publication Data

Names: Beth, Georgia, author.
Title: STEM. Building tiny houses / Georgia Beth.
Description: Huntington Beach, CA : Teacher Created Materials, 2018. | Includes index. | Audience: K to Grade 3. |
Identifiers: LCCN 2017049147 (print) | LCCN 2017049817 (ebook) | ISBN 9781425859480 (eBook) | ISBN 9781425857585 (pbk.)
Subjects: LCSH: Architecture--Composition, proportion, etc.--Juvenile literature. | Small houses--Juvenile literature.
Classification: LCC NA2760 (ebook) | LCC NA2760 .B45 2018 (print) | DDC 728/.37--dc23
LC record available at https://lccn.loc.gov/2017049147

Teacher Created Materials

5301 Oceanus Drive
Huntington Beach, CA 92649-1030
http://www.tcmpub.com

ISBN 978-1-4258-5758-5

© 2018 Teacher Created Materials, Inc.
Printed in China WAI002

Table of Contents

Home Sweet Home

People say that home is where the heart is. That means that they do not need a big house if they live with people they love. In fact, some people like to live in tiny houses. A tiny house looks like a regular house. But it is much smaller. Most tiny houses are less than 20 feet (6 meters) long. That is about the size of a large living room! It may seem small, but tiny-house owners feel right at home in these little spaces.

tiny house

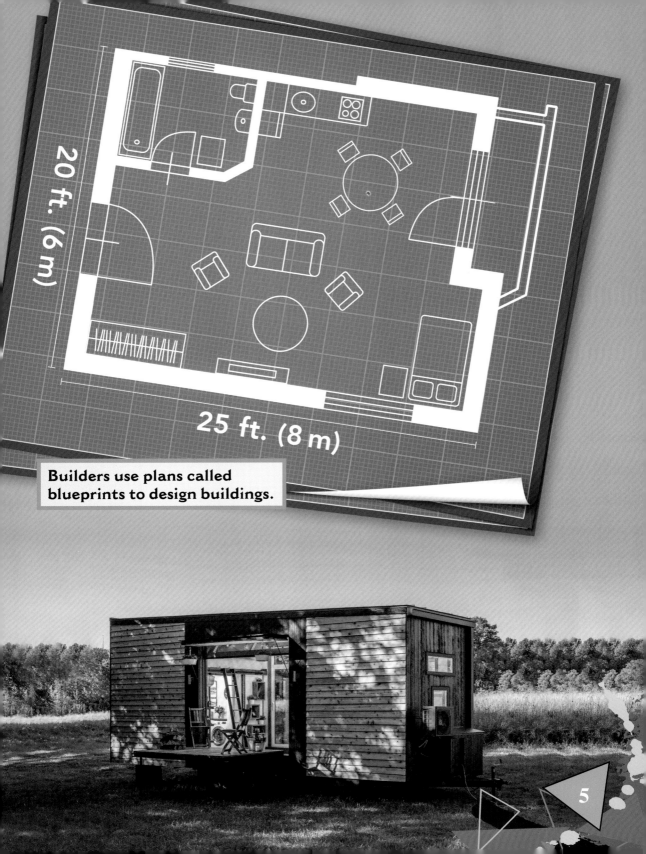

20 ft. (6 m)

25 ft. (8 m)

Builders use plans called
blueprints to design buildings.

Tiny House, Big Idea

Living in tiny houses gives people a chance to live big lives. Small homes cost less. They create less **waste**, too. So, tiny-house owners can live where land costs more. Many choose to live near nature. Others use their money to travel. Some people even bring their houses with them!

Some tiny-house owners choose to live by the ocean.

This tiny house can sleep up to eight people.

Building the Basics

People save money by buying tiny houses. They can save even more if they build their own house.

When people build their own houses, they can choose what they want to put in each room. As they build, they think of ways to make their small spaces feel huge.

People work together to build a tiny house.

Imagine the new owners of a tiny house are decorating it.

1. The owners of the house have a footrest shaped like a cube. They want to make a new covering for it by sewing together fabric squares. How many squares do they need to use to cover all sides? How do you know?

2. A window in the house is shaped like a triangle. The owners want to hang a straight curtain rod across it. They want the window to be divided into a trapezoid and a smaller triangle. Draw a triangle similar to the one below. Show where the owners should hang the curtain rod.

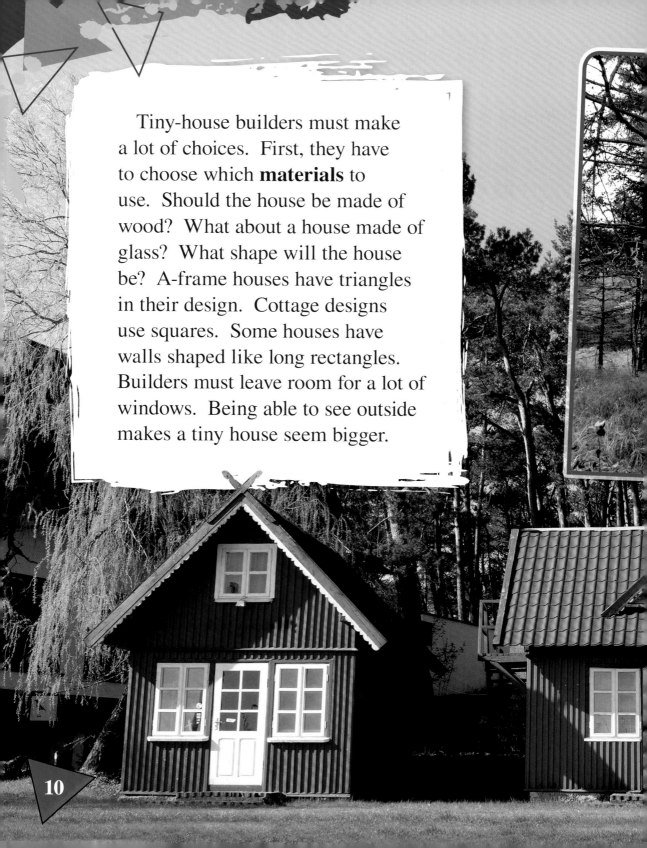

Tiny-house builders must make a lot of choices. First, they have to choose which **materials** to use. Should the house be made of wood? What about a house made of glass? What shape will the house be? A-frame houses have triangles in their design. Cottage designs use squares. Some houses have walls shaped like long rectangles. Builders must leave room for a lot of windows. Being able to see outside makes a tiny house seem bigger.

This tiny house is made of wood.

After they build the outside of a house, builders look at **floor plans**. These plans show where each room will go. They show builders the shape of each room. Builders make sure all the pieces of a tiny house fit together. They try new things. Will a triangle sink take up less room than a square sink? Can the bed be round? The answers to questions like these help builders decide what to do.

This floor plan shows the different areas of a tiny house.

The builder of a tiny house is ready to tile the kitchen floor. The floor is a rectangle.

1. Draw a rectangle similar to the one below. Show how the builder can use square tiles to cover the floor.

2. The owners of the house change their mind. They want the kitchen floor to be covered in rectangles instead of squares. Draw another rectangle. Show how the builder can use rectangle tiles to cover the floor.

Two builders plan where to hammer a nail.

13

A man sits in his loft bedroom.

Tiny houses are not long or wide. But, they can be tall. High ceilings and second floors add space. Shelves and **loft** bedrooms give a lot of options for a small space. Some tiny houses have ladders to the lofts. Tiny-house owners cannot build out. So, they have to think of new ways to build up.

A builder installs shelves that look like hexagons. The owners want the shelves divided into display units.

1. Draw a hexagon similar to those shown. Show how it can be divided into trapezoids.

2. The owners want to see other ideas. Draw another hexagon. Show how it can be divided into triangles.

3. How can the builder divide a hexagon into a combination of triangles and trapezoids? Draw to show your solution.

Being **creative** is part of the fun of living in a tiny house. People might store tools under the stairs. They might store their clothes under their beds. They might use their beds as chairs. They might even put windows in their roofs if there is not enough space on the walls. That way, they can let in daylight and look at the stars at night.

This bed has hidden storage and can be pushed under the kitchen floor.

This man's tiny home has a TV room below his office and bedroom.

This house was built on a rock in the middle of a river.

Making It Your Own

Many tiny-house owners have never lived in such a small space. They may not know where to start. Designers can help. They make sure the house is built just the way owners want it.

Designers can make houses **permanent**. Or, they can help owners take their houses on the road. That way, they can always have a roof over their heads!

Imagine you are a tiny-house designer. The homeowners want a big window in their living room.

1. How many square pieces of glass make up the window?

2. What is the shape of the large window formed by the square pieces of glass?

Designers do not just work on the outsides of houses. They can make the insides look great, too. Many designers start by asking what owners like to do. Then, they make space for the owners' **hobbies**.

If owners like to paint, they can ask for a shelf for their paints. If they like to watch TV, they can hide their TVs behind sliding walls. These small changes can make a house feel like a home.

This tiny house has a TV that can be hidden when not in use.

This tiny house has shelves for storage.

a tiny house with solar panels

Smart or Strange?

Living in a tiny house means finding new ways to **solve** problems. Some people add fabric to the insides of their walls. That helps keep houses warm. Some people add **solar panels** or gardens to their roofs. That way, they can use the sun to light their houses and grow food.

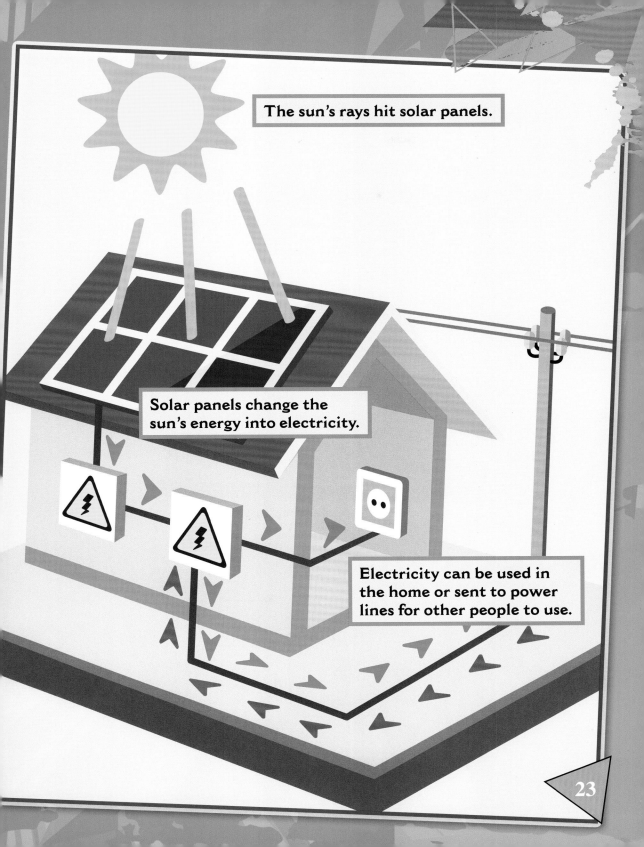

The sun's rays hit solar panels.

Solar panels change the sun's energy into electricity.

Electricity can be used in the home or sent to power lines for other people to use.

23

People use light colors to make houses look bigger. Light things, such as white walls and chairs, can make houses feel less tiny. Black will make rooms feel small. So, most people do not use a lot of dark colors. Some people get creative and paint rainbows on their walls. One trick is to make the walls round. Then, tiny-house owners will not feel like they live in small boxes.

White walls
are common
in tiny houses.

Welcome Home!

   Could you live in a tiny house? Would you take it on the road, or would you set up your home next to a lake? With a tiny house, you can live any place you want. You can spend the summer by the beach. Then, you can move to the mountains when it gets cold. Not everyone will like living in a tiny house. But if you design, plan, and build it the way you want, your tiny house might be your dream house.

This tiny house is on wheels, so the owners can move whenever they want.

This tiny house in Germany has a ladder to reach the bedroom.

⚙ Problem Solving

Imagine you are planning to build a tiny house. You have chosen the shape of each room. Now, you need to fit the rooms together to make floor plans. Use the shapes shown to answer the prompts below for your tiny house.

1. The first floor of your house will be a rectangle. Draw a rectangular floor plan using the kitchen, bathroom, workspace, and closet.

2. The bedroom will be a second-floor loft.

   a. Name the shape of the bedroom floor.

   b. The bedroom will be divided into three areas: one for sleeping, one for reading, and one for working on the computer. Show a way to divide the space into three shapes, and name each shape.

3. The rooftop will feature a garden.

   a. Name the shape of the garden.

   b. The garden will have plots for vegetables and flowers. Show a way to divide the floor plan into two square plots for vegetables and two triangle plots for flowers.

bedroom

workspace

kitchen

closet

bathroom

garden

Glossary

creative—able to think of new ideas or make new things

floor plans—drawings that show the placement of rooms in buildings

hobbies—activities done for fun

lofts—an open area that is on the upper floor of a building

materials—things that can be used to make or build other things

permanent—not movable or changing

solar panels—large, flat pieces of equipment that use the sun's heat or light to create electricity

solve—find an answer to a problem

waste—something that is left over and cannot be used

Index

Answer Key

Let's Explore Math

page 9:

1. 6 squares; answers will vary but may include that all cubes are made up of 6 squares.

2.

page 13:

1. Drawings will vary. Example:

2. Drawings will vary. Example:

page 15:

1. Drawings will vary. Example:

2. Drawings will vary. Example:

3. Drawings will vary. Example:

page 19:

1. 15 square pieces of glass

2. rectangle; quadrilateral; parallelogram

Problem Solving

1.

2. **a.** trapezoid

   b. Answers will vary but should have three shapes with each shape labeled.

3. **a.** rectangle

   b. Answers will vary. Example: